ELEMENTS OF DRAMA

Elements of Drama

ROBERT SCHOLES
BROWN UNIVERSITY

CARL H. KLAUS
UNIVERSITY OF IOWA

New York
Oxford University Press
London 1971 Toronto

Copyright © 1971 by Oxford University Press, Inc.

Library of Congress Catalogue Card Number: 78-82991

From *Endgame* by Samuel Beckett. Copyright © 1958 by Grove Press, Inc. Reprinted by permission of Grove Press, Inc., and Faber & Faber Ltd.

From *The Misanthrope*, by Molière, translated by Richard Wilbur, © copyright 1954, 1955 by Richard Wilbur. Reprinted by permission of Harcourt Brace Jovanovich, Inc., and Faber & Faber Ltd.

From *Oedipus Rex: An English Version* by Dudley Fitts and Robert Fitzgerald, copyright 1949 by Harcourt Brace Jovanovich, Inc. Reprinted by permission of Harcourt Brace Jovanovich, Inc., and Faber & Faber Ltd.

Printed in the United States of America

ON THE NATURE AND PURPOSE OF THIS TEXT

All too often drama is considered to be either literature or theater. Literature departments take one approach, theater departments the other. Actually, drama incorporates literary *and* theatrical art. And with this book we hope to encourage the study of drama in relation to both literary and theatrical contexts. Thus we have devoted the first part of our book to explaining these contexts and the way they interact to produce the unique experience of drama. In the remaining parts of our study, we discuss the modes and elements of drama in terms of the interaction between these contexts.

Our discussion of drama is illustrated primarily, though not exclusively, by reference to four plays: *Oedipus Rex*, *A Midsummer-Night's Dream*, *The Misanthrope*, and *Endgame*. We have chosen these plays for several reasons. They were written at four different periods for four entirely different theaters: the classical Greek, the renaissance English, the neo-classical French, and the modern. At the same time, they show very clearly the way that drama is related to the other literary forms: essay, fiction, and poetry. Furthermore, they embody in various ways the dominant modes of drama: romance and satire, comedy and tragedy. Last but not least, they are great plays by great dramatists: Sophocles, Shakespeare, Molière, and Beckett. Thus we urge that they be read *before* the reading of this text.

CONTENTS

ELEMENTS OF DRAMA

PART ONE

CONTEXTS OF DRAMA

I DRAMA, LITERATURE, AND REPRESENTATIONAL ART

Drama begins in make-believe, in the play acting of children, in the ritual of primitive religion. And it never forsakes its primitive beginnings, for imitative action is its essence. When an actor appears on stage, he makes believe he is someone other than himself, much as a child does, much as primitive people still do. Thus like play-acting and ritual, drama creates its experience by doing things that can be heard and seen. "Drama," in fact, comes from a Greek word which means "thing done." And the things it does, as with play-acting and ritual, create a world apart—a world modelled on our own, but one which has its own charmed existence.

Drama, of course, is neither primitive ritual nor child's play, but it does share with them the essential quality of enactment. This quality should remind us that drama is not solely a form of literature. It is at once literary art *and* representational art. As literary art, a play is a fiction made out of words. It has a plot,

characters, and dialogue. But it is a special kind of
fiction—a fiction *acted out* rather than narrated. Thus
in a novel or short story, we learn about characters and
events through the words of a narrator who stands
between us and them. But in a play nothing stands
between us and the total make-up of its world. Characters appear and events happen without any inter-
mediate comment or explanation. Drama, then, offers
us a *direct* presentation of its reality. In this sense it is
representational art.

As students of drama, this faces us with something
of a paradox. Because it is literature, a play can be
read. But because it is representational art, a play is
meant to be witnessed. We can see this problem in
other terms. The text of a play is like the score of a
symphony—a finished work, yet only a potentiality
until it is performed. Most plays are written to be performed. Those eccentric few that are not—that are
written only to be read—we usually refer to as "closet
dramas." Very little can take place in a closet, but
anything is possible in the theater, from the fairies of
A Midsummer-Night's Dream to the garbage cans of
Endgame. The magic of theater, its ability to conjure
up such incredible worlds, depends on the power of
spectacle. And by spectacle we mean all the sights and
sounds of performance—the slightest twitch or the
boldest thrust of a sword, the faintest whisper or the
loudest cry.

But for most of us the experience of drama is usually

confined to plays in print rather than performance. This means that we have to be unusually resourceful in our study of drama. Careful reading is not enough. We have to be creative readers as well. Like the dramatist who writes the play, we have to imagine it on the stage. Thus not only must we attend to the meanings and implications of words. We also have to envision the words in performance. Can you imagine what it looks and sounds like when Oedipus accuses Teiresias, or Titania woos Bottom, or Alceste insults Oronte, or Clov awakens Hamm?

By asking such questions, we actually force ourselves to struggle with the same problems that directors and actors face when they stage a play. And by taking on those problems, we can then begin to experience the understanding *and* pleasure that spectators gain when they attend a play. Thus as readers, we want to put ourselves in the place of directors, actors, and spectators. Their place, of course, is the theater, where our study properly begins.

II DRAMA AND THE SHAPE OF THEATERS

Theaters are designed for the staging and witnessing of plays. Their function has never changed. But their shape has, and every change has produced a different kind of dramatic experience. This is so, because the shape of a theater affects everyone involved in the making of drama. Dramatists, for example, are influenced by the physical characteristics of the stage for which they are writing, actors by the size of the audience to which they are playing, and spectators by the point of view from which they are watching. These are only a few of the ways that the form of a theater can determine the nature of a dramatic experience, and you can easily imagine others by remembering how in *A Midsummer-Night's Dream*, Quince and his fellows go about producing their play, or by noticing how Theseus and his guests respond to it. As a dramatist, of course, Shakespeare was intensely aware of the theatrical situation, so much so that he knew how to poke fun at it in the play within his play. But the comedy depends on our knowing something about the Elizabethan stage. Similarly, our understanding of any play depends on knowing about the theater for which it was originally written and produced. Remembering this, we will begin by looking at four kinds of theaters and the unique experience of each kind.

The Classical Greek Theater. Its extraordinary size is what immediately strikes us about the ancient Greek theater. The theater of Dionysus at Athens, where *Oedipus Rex* was first produced (*c.* 425 B.C.), could accommodate an audience of almost 14,000; the theater at Epidaurus, 20,000; and the theater of Ephesus, more than 50,000. Structures so large were, of course, not closed, but open-air. These facts alone will take us a long way toward understanding the nature of a Greek dramatic performance. To begin with, we can see that the experience must have been very public and communal—nothing at all like the coziness of our fully enclosed modern theaters, where no more than 500 to 1000 gather in darkened rows of cushioned seats. The size of the Greek theater also meant that drama had to be conceived in monumental terms and executed in a correspondingly emphatic style of acting. When Oedipus accused Teiresias of treason, his impetuous judgment had to be heard and seen by thousands of spectators. Facial expressions obviously would not serve the purpose, nor would conversational tones. Instead, the actors wore large stylized masks and costumes—an inheritance from primitive ritual—representing generalized character types. And their masks were probably equipped with mouthpieces to aid in the projection of dialogue. Thus we should not imagine a style of performance in any way corresponding to our present-day standards of dramatic realism. Exaggerated gestures, bold movements, declamatory utterances—everything was larger than life and highly formalized, if only to assure a clear theatrical impression.

But size alone was not responsible for the highly formal art of Greek drama. The shape of things, and the religious heritage of the theater's shape, also had a great deal to do with the ceremonial nature of the experience. The Greek theater emerged from places of ritual celebration which consisted of a circular area for dancers and singers surrounded by a hillside to accommodate worshippers. A modified version of that arrangement is what we have in the Greek theater:

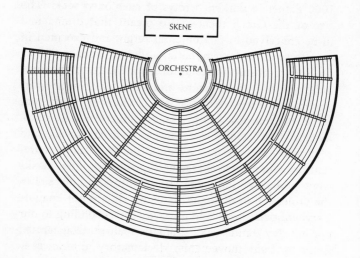

The *skene* (scene building), a one-story structure used to store properties and change costumes, provided three doors for entrances and exits. Stylized scenes were painted on the areas between the doors to suggest the general outlines of a location, and the *skene* itself represented any building central to the action, such as the palace in Oedipus. Other than these few hints, the Greek stage provided very little scenery to assist the spectator's imagination. At the most, a chariot might be driven in to the *orchestra* to represent the arrival of a hero, or an actor lowered by machine from the roof of the *skene* to depict the intervention of a god, or a tableau pulled on wheels from inside the *skene* to suggest offstage action.

The most important part of the theater was the *orchestra*. This circular space, eighty-five feet in diameter, served as the primary acting area. The actors entered it directly from the *skene;* the chorus entered it through the passageways in front of the audience. Once they had entered, the chorus remained in the *orchestra* throughout the performance. Thus the chorus provided a continual point of reference to mediate between the audience and the actors. The actors, however, moved back and forth between the *orchestra* and the *skene* as their parts dictated.

In trying to imagine the effect produced by the simultaneous presence of actors and chorus, it is important to remember that the chorus retained the skills that originated with the ritual celebrations of an earlier time. Thus the members of the chorus, like the actors, were highly accomplished dancers and singers. And each type of play had a corresponding type of dance movement and song. When we read *Oedipus*

Rex, for example, we should try to imagine what it looked like as the chorus moved through its slow and graceful dance appropriate to tragedy. And we should try to imagine what it sounded like as the chorus, accompanied by a flute player, sang its parts, sometimes written for one voice, sometimes for two, sometimes for the entire group of fifteen that figures in Sophocles' plays. Obviously, the total performance must have been as musically and visually complex as a modern-day opera, yet not quite the same, for in opera everything is subordinated to the music and song, whereas in Greek drama all was subordinated to the action.

The Renaissance English Theater. Shakespeare's theater is different in almost all respects from the Greek. To begin with it was considerably smaller. Estimates of its capacity vary from 2000 to 3000, but these figures are enough to suggest that it provided a completely different experience for the spectators. The Globe, where many of Shakespeare's plays were performed, was an octagonally shaped building, eighty-four feet in diameter, and thirty-three feet high. Inside the theater there were three galleries for spectators. The remaining area was only fifty-five feet in diameter. Into this space extended a stage forty-three feet wide and about twenty-seven feet deep. The ground area surrounding the stage was also filled with spectators. On the basis of these dimensions, we can visualize something like this:

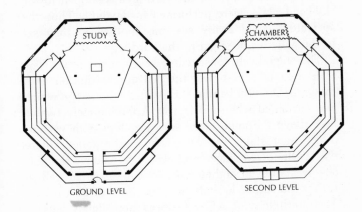

GROUND LEVEL   SECOND LEVEL

Immediately we can see that this arrangement must have created a much more intimate relation between actors and spectators than was possible in the Greek theater. Since the actors were closely surrounded on three sides by spectators in the yard and the galleries, their acting style was correspondingly more natural than the Greek. This closeness also meant that the actors had to pay meticulous attention to all of their gestures and facial expressions. And most significantly, perhaps, the physical intimacy necessarily aroused in the spectators a very immediate and personal engagement in the experience of the play—much greater certainly than was possible in the Greek theater. But in another respect, we can see that the theater was still a very public affair, for the yard area was open to the sky, and plays were performed in daylight. Thus the spectators could easily see one another as they sat in the galleries or stood in the yard.

The stage itself consisted of seven acting areas. The main area, of course, was the platform jutting out into the yard. Directly behind this was an inner stage which was curtained when not in use. Approximately twelve feet above the main stage was a gallery with yet another inner stage. On each side of the gallery there was a windowed stage. And eleven feet above the gallery was an even higher stage for musicians as well as for special scenes located on a masthead or in a tower. The multiplicity of acting surfaces immediately tells us that Shakespeare was writing in terms of an extraordinarily flexible theater, allowing numerous and rapid changes in location.

On the other hand, evidence seems to suggest that scenery was not in use, and only a few props were available to suggest the location of a scene—a bed, a chair, a tree, and so on. Costuming apparently was sumptuous, but by no means authentic. In fact, most actors wore costumes designed according to Elizabethan styles of dress. Thus the Elizabethan theater made no serious attempt to create anything like the complete physical illusion we are accustomed to on the modern stage. As a result, the dramatists depended heavily upon the imaginations of their audience. And the audience depended heavily on the suggestiveness of the dialogue. These circumstances required a richness of language that we find throughout Shakespeare's plays. Consider, for example, some of the forest scenes in *A Midsummer-Night's Dream*, and you will see how Shakespeare is able to evoke the sense of a complete and richly complicated landscape without having to depend on the elaborate sets, machines, and lighting effects of the modern theater. And if you look again at the scenes in which the "mechanicals" are rehearsing and producing their play, you will probably be able to understand the private theatrical jokes that Shakespeare is making when Bottom, Quince, and the others worry about the props for their performance.

The Neo-Classical French Theater. Molière's and Shakespeare's theaters are as different as night and day. In fact, the theater of the Palais Royal, where most of Molière's plays were performed between 1660 and 1670, was a fully enclosed structure within the elegant palace originally built by Cardinal Richelieu. Thus daylight was replaced by candlelight. But this is only one of a wide range of differences all of which anticipate later developments in theatrical design.

Perhaps the most important breaks with the past can be seen in the shape of the theater and the physical relation between the actors and audience. The theater of the Palais Royal was designed in the shape

of a long rectangle. At one end was a relatively deep
stage equipped with a proscenium arch. Several steps
led down from the stage to the auditorium, and a
greater number gradually moved upwards to the back
of the hall. The steps leading up to the lobby were
equipped with wooden seats, and on each side of the
hall there were two levels of galleries for spectators.
The total capacity of the theater was 600. Thus
Molière's audience attended a theater shaped like this:

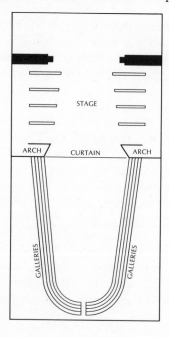

On the basis of the diagram we can immediately see how radically different this theater is from those of Shakespeare and Sophocles. The spectators do not surround the acting area. Instead, they witness the play from a single perspective, as if they were looking into a box, one side of which has been stripped away. Furthermore, the spectators, despite the relatively small size of the theater, no longer have the kind of intimate relation to the actors that was made possible on the Elizabethan stage. Actors and spectators are clearly divided from one another by the proscenium arch which frames the play like a picture. And the barrier created by the arch was increased by the use of a curtain to divide the acts.

In addition to its physical layout, the theater of the Palais Royal differs from the Greek and Elizabethan in the complicated scenic devices and stage machinery with which it was equipped. The action of *The Misanthrope*, for example, was played in front of a scene depicting the interior of Célimène's house. Thus we can see the stage being altered to suit the interest of creating a visual illusion. But illusion was not the only function served by the scenes and machines. They also satisfied a growing fascination with spectacular effects as an end in themselves. Molière, for example, on the order of the king, wrote a play, *The Bores*, which opened with no less than twenty natural fountains spouting water, followed by the appearance of an actress who emerged from a large sea shell to recite her prologue. Even *The Misanthrope* was not free of such bizarre goings-on. Thus the audience that witnessed the play was treated not only to the action itself, but also to ballet interludes accompanied by appropriate scenic changes.

Acting styles of the period were highly formalized. If we try to imagine the style used in *The Misanthrope* we will do best to turn to *commedia dell'arte*, a popular form of drama which emerged during the Italian Renaissance (16th century), and which exerted a strong influence on French actors, particularly on Molière. *Commedia* was a highly improvisational theater built up out of an array of type characters, such as the clever servant, the braggart soldier, the ingenious maid, the foolish husband, the angry father, and so on. Associated with each of the types was a stylized and exaggerated mode of gesture and movement. Can you imagine how such actors might play the parts of Arsinoé (the hypocritical prude), or Célimène (the flirtatious coquette), or Oronte (the vain fop)? Even if you have difficulty with this problem, you can easily see how the style of *commedia* would fit perfectly the satiric purposes of Molière.

The Modern Theater. Most of us are familiar with it in one form or another, and it can take many shapes indeed. But for our immediate purposes it is probably best to deal first with the most common type—the one we might find on Broadway or on our local campus.

The audience is separated from the actors by the proscenium arch, and the barrier is further intensified by the use of lighting focused exclusively on the stage; the audience sits in total darkness. Although the effects of this are momentous, we often fail to realize them. No longer is the experience public or communal. Each member of the audience is separated from the others by the darkness that surrounds him. Thus the experience is private rather than public—individual rather than communal. Furthermore, the combination of darkness and light places the audience in the position of snoopers or spies, looking in on characters who are presumably unaware that they are being watched. The actors, for example, go through their gestures and motions as if the space defined by the arch did not exist, as if they were in a room surrounded by four walls. And this illusion is richly sustained by the highly realistic scenes and props of the modern stage. As a result of these conditions, the modern dramatist need not depend on his language to evoke the sense of a world. He need only, as does Beckett, write directions to be followed by the set designer.

Although these modern developments have in one sense made it easier for the audience to enter into the imaginative world of drama, they have at the same time made it harder for the audience to extend its imagination beyond the detailed visual illusion of the stage. After all, the audience that depends exclusively on its eyes is likely to be as blind as Oedipus before he discovered another way of seeing. Recognizing this, a number of contemporary dramatists, drama critics, and theater architects have rediscovered the older shape of things. Thus we are likely to find theaters nowadays that abandon the proscenium arch in favor of theater in the round, or a modified version of the multiple stages in Shakespeare's playhouse, or a semi-circular amphitheater style approximating the Greek stage.

Theaters such as these depend less upon visual props and more upon the suggestive power of deeds and words. Responding to these suggestions, we can imagine a much larger world that is contained within the box of a proscenium stage. We can, in fact, imagine a world without limits—an open-ended world such as Shakespeare offers us in *A Midsummer-Night's Dream.* In this way, we may indeed be able to recapture the theatrical experience of the past and renew the theatrical life of the present.

III   DRAMA AND OTHER LITERARY FORMS

Up to this point we have considered drama primarily as a theatrical event—a representational art to be performed and witnessed. In doing so, we have been concerned with the uniquely dramatic experience which is possible only on the stage. But it should be remembered that any performance, moving as it may be, is an interpretation—of how the lines should be performed, stressing some words, minimizing others, including some meanings, excluding others. Thus every performance of a play, even by the same actors, represents a different realization of its possibilities, and no single performance can fully realize all of its possibilities. All the possibilities exist in its language. This should remind us that drama is a form of literature—an art made out of words. It should be understood, then, in relation not only to the theater, but also to the other literary forms: essay, story, and poem.

In relating drama to other literary forms, we can begin by considering how words are used and communicated in literature. Essentially we can say that words are used either to create plots and characters, or to express ideas and feelings. In defining how words are communicated, we can observe that they are either addressed directly to the reader, as in a rhetorical situation, or overheard by him, as in a poetic situation. With these basic possibilities in mind, we can draw a simple coordinate system, like this:

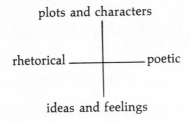

plots and characters

rhetorical ——————— poetic

ideas and feelings

The vertical axis refers to the way words are used, the horizontal axis to the manner in which words are communicated to the reader. Thus within the coordinates, we can locate each literary form according to the unique way it employs words and communicates them to the reader.

The essay in its purest form uses words to establish ideas addressed directly by the essayist to the reader. On this basis we can see that its essential quality is persuasion and that it belongs in the lower left-hand area of the diagram. The poem in its purest form uses words to express feelings addressed by a speaker talking or thinking to himself rather than to the reader. Its essential quality, then, is meditation, and it belongs in the lower right-hand area of the diagram. A story uses words to develop a view of character and situation through the report of a story-teller to the reader. Its essential quality is narration, and it belongs in the upper left-hand area. And a play uses words to create action through the dialogue of characters talking to one another rather than to the reader. Thus the essential quality of drama is interaction, and it belongs in the upper right-hand area of the diagram. Once the forms and their qualities have been defined and located, the diagram looks like this:

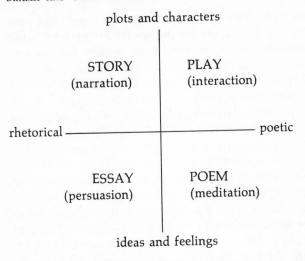

With this diagram and the accompanying definitions, we can visualize immediately the unique literary quality of drama as distinguished from the other forms. But the diagram can take us further in our study if we realize that it also represents the closeness of the four forms to one another. Within each of the literary forms all four possibilities exist again as emphases or strategies. Thus a play, although it depends primarily on the interaction of dialogue, can also use the techniques and assume the qualities of the other forms. As the diagram indicates, drama has affinities with the story in its use of language, and connections with the poem in its communication of language. Like the story it is

concerned with plot and character, and like the
poem it is overheard by the reader rather than being
addressed directly to him. And though the diagram
reveals that drama does not have a close connection
with the essay, it is not unusual for a play to assume
the persuasive quality we associate with the essay.
Using these relationships as points of departure, we
can now examine some of the ways that drama takes
on the characteristics and devices of the other forms.

Drama and Narration. A play is most dramatic, of
course, when it uses the give and take of dialogue to
create interaction. But the interaction always takes
place within a specific context—a background in time
and place without which it cannot be properly understood. To develop this kind of understanding drama
turns to the narrative techniques of the story. This is
not to say that we should expect to find storytellers
addressing us directly in plays. Occasionally they do
turn up, but more often the characters themselves become storytellers in their dialogue with one another.
The most obvious form of this story-telling occurs at
the beginning of plays and is appropriately called exposition, for it sets forth and explains in a manner
typical of narrative. This is the case, for example, in
the address of the Priest at the opening of *Oedipus:*

> Thebes is in her extremity
> And can not lift her head from the surge of death.
> A rust consumes the buds and fruits of the earth;

The herds are sick, children die unborn,
And labor is vain. The god of plague and pyre
Raids like detestable lightning through the city,
And all the house of Kadmos is laid waste,
All emptied, and all darkened: Death alone
Battens upon the misery of Thebes.

You are not one of the immortal gods, we know;
Yet we have come to you to make our prayer
As to the wisest in the ways of God. You saved us
From the Sphinx, that flinty singer, and the tribute
We paid to her so long; yet you were never
Better informed than we, nor could we teach you:
It was some god breathed in you to set us free.

Clearly enough this is a dramatic plea for help, and its power depends both on the vision of horror as well as the tribute to Oedipus. But the appeal is so elaborately drawn out that it also serves to give us essential background and to formulate a point of view toward Oedipus. Thus we get both a visual evocation of the setting (this is important in a theater without scenery and props), which explains the source of the crisis, and an important piece of information about Oedipus, which immediately establishes his heroic stature for us. In this case, interaction and narration go hand in hand, one purpose serving the other.

Related to exposition is another narrative feature we call retrospection. Often during the process of action, characters will look back and survey important events

which took place well before the play began, and when
this happens drama is again using a device of narration. Retrospection, of course, is a recurrent element
in *Oedipus Rex*, for we can notice Jocasta, Oedipus,
and the Shepherd successively reviewing incidents in
their past lives. Can you explain how their story-
telling determines and gives meaning to the interaction
of the play? The counterpart of retrospection is foreshadowing, when one of the characters anticipates and
reports what the outcome of the whole play, or some
part of it, will be. Teiresias does this in *Oedipus Rex*.
Can you imagine why Sophocles, or any other dramatist, would be willing to give away this information?
Retrospection and foreshadowing are not unique to
Oedipus Rex. Shakespeare, for example, frequently
uses these narrative devices in *A Midsummer-Night's
Dream*, but in doing so he obviously achieves different
effects from Sophocles'. As a valuable exercise in reading, you might want to review these two plays, con-
centrating solely on retrospection and foreshadowing
to see how in each case similar narrative devices can
have quite different effects on the action.

Up to this point we have looked at narrative elements which refer to pre-play action or subsequent
action in the play itself. But we can also notice occasions in drama when narration takes over completely,
when it replaces interaction. Occasions such as these
are produced by offstage action which is reported
rather than represented, and when this happens the

play becomes most nearly like a story—words are being used to develop a view of character and situation rather than to create action through dialogue. We can see this process most clearly in the extended speech of the Second Messenger when he tells the Chorus about the death of Jocasta and the self-blinding of Oedipus. The interaction on stage ceases entirely for the length of almost fifty lines, and what we get instead has all the features of a miniature story. The Messenger begins by establishing his narrative authority: ". . . what happened you can not know, / For you did not see it; but I, who did, will tell you / As clearly as I can how she met her death." Then he moves into his tale, "When she had left us," supplying information, "She ran to her apartment in the house . . . She closed the doors behind her . . . We heard her call upon Laios," acknowledging and explaining omissions, "Exactly how she died I do not know: / For Oedipus burst in moaning and would not let us keep vigil to the end," making narrative transitions, "it was by him . . . that our eyes were caught," offering interpretations, "I do not know: it was none of us aided him, / But surely one of the gods was in control," reporting dialogue, and concluding with general reflections:

So from the unhappiness of two this evil has sprung,
A curse on the man and woman alike. The old
Happiness of the house of Labdakos
Was happiness enough: where is it today?

It is all wailing and ruin, disgrace, death—all
The misery of mankind that has a name—
And it is wholly and for ever theirs.

In trying to explain why Sophocles chooses to have
these events reported rather than show them on stage,
it is natural to say that they are too gruesome to be
displayed. And certainly this is true. But it is also true
that the Messenger's report of events enables Sophocles to introduce a commentary on their meaning.
Ordinarily this kind of reflection is available only to
the narrator of a story. To achieve similar effects the
dramatist must turn to messengers or other functionaries who are not involved in the action, and can,
therefore, comment upon it. The Second Messenger's
commentary at this point makes a poignant reversal
of the Priest's remarks of the beginning, for we recall
that the Priest could only see the "misery of Thebes"
and the godlike wisdom of Oedipus, whereas now the
Messenger can see that "all the misery of mankind"
springs from Oedipus and Jocasta—"wholly and for-
ever theirs."

As we have already indicated, Sophocles is by no
means the only dramatist to use narrative techniques.
Reported action can be found at a number of points in
A Midsummer-Night's Dream. One of the more unusual examples takes place immediately after the actions which show Bottom acquiring the ass's head and
Titania's love. At this point Puck delivers a lengthy

and elaborate report of these same events to Oberon. The report is justified, of course, by Oberon's need to be informed, but it also serves the purpose of giving these episodes plausibility through repetition, not to mention the additional laughter that comes from savoring the comedy again. Later in the play, Bottom and Titania, upon awakening from their trance, also report their impressions of the same earlier events, and their differing perspectives create a further source of comedy. Thus reported action can serve a variety of functions, and it can even refer to interaction which has already been represented in the play.

In discussing reported action, we have seen how the Second Messenger moved from story-telling to commentary, and this brings us to the last important element of narration in drama—choric commentary. When the narrator of a story wishes to suspend the action in order to comment or generalize on characters and events, he can do so at will. But the dramatist, of course, cannot suddenly appear in the play—or on stage—to provide a point of view on the action. The dramatist's alternative is the chorus or choric characters—personages, that is, who are relatively detached from the action, and can, therefore, stand off from it, somewhat like a narrator, to reflect on the significance of events. In Greek drama, the chorus performed this function, and the detachment of the chorus was theatrically manifested by its continuous presence in the orchestra. Thus the chorus literally stood between the audience and the action, much as a narrator stands between the reader and the story. But the position of the chorus does not mean that its opinions are always to be trusted. Sometimes it can be as wrongheaded as any of the more involved characters. Certainly this is the case when the chorus in *Oedipus Rex* repudiates Teiresias' prophecies, insisting that his "evil words are lies." At other times, the chorus is completely reliable, as in its concluding remarks about the frailty of the human condition. Choric commentary, then, provides a point of view, but not necessarily an authoritative one, nor one to be associated with the dramatist. In each case, the commentary has to be examined as closely as any other material in the play. In the first instance we have cited, Sophocles is using the chorus to project what we might call public opinion which would naturally be sympathetic to Oedipus and legitimately shocked by the accusations and prophecies of Teiresias. Whereas in the second case, the Chorus is being used to express the wisdom that any thoughtful person would draw from the experience of Oedipus.

After the classical Greek period, the formal chorus disappeared almost entirely from drama. Remnants of the chorus can, of course, be found in later plays— even in contemporary drama. But for us as readers the important matter is to recognize that choric characters persist in drama despite the absence of a formally designated chorus. Dramatic functionaries, such as messengers, servants, clowns, or others not directly involved in the action, can carry out the functions of a chorus, and the attitudes they express should be examined for the point of view they provide on the action. Thus Puck, who serves Oberon, and the Fairies, who serve Titania, have choric roles in *A Midsummer-Night's Dream*. Characters otherwise involved in the action can also take on the temporary status of choric commentators, particularly if circumstances permit them to stand off and formulate a point of view. We can see this happen when Quince and his fellows finally produce their play. At this point, Theseus and his guests become spectators whose responses have a choric significance which applies not only to the play they are watching, but to *A Midsummer-Night's Dream* as well. Theseus, for example, in defending the rustic players remarks that "The best in this kind are but shadows: and the worst are no worse, if imagination amend them," reminding us of the special imaginative effort we must make in witnessing any theatrical production, whether it be Quince's or Shakespeare's. Once we recognize that any character can become a spectator of his world, then it is possible to see that Philinte in *The Misanthrope* and Clov in *Endgame* are also choric commentators of a sort. Philinte, for example, offers us a persistently critical view of Alceste, and Clov provides a similar perspective on Hamm. Granting this to be true, can you see any reasons why Philinte and Clov might not be considered choric characters?

Drama and Meditation. If we remember that interaction through dialogue is the basis of drama, then we can readily see that a play is by its very nature committed to showing us the public side of its characters. The same thing is true in real life. When we are conversing with someone, we show the public side of our personality. The private side we keep to ourselves. In private we do not even use our voice, for meditation is essentially a silent activity which we carry on within ourselves. Only then is the mind free to have its own way, to entertain any idea or feeling, unhampered by the demands of conversation. Realizing this, we can see the artistic problem a dramatist faces when he wants to show the private side of his characters. The narrator of a story can solve this problem by taking the liberty of telling us about the innermost thoughts of his characters, and even then we must be willing to concede that it is possible for him to have this special kind of knowledge. But in order for the dramatist to show the intimate feelings of characters, he must turn to the conventions of the poem, using words addressed by a speaker talking or thinking to himself. In reading a purely lyric poem, we automatically assume that the situation is private rather than public and that it is possible for us to overhear the words even though they might never be spoken aloud. In reading or witnessing a play, we must make a similar imaginative effort. To assist our efforts, dramatists have traditionally organized their plays to make sure that a character thinking to himself is seen in privacy. Thus the origin of our term "soliloquy" which means literally to speak alone. But it is also true that we do have private thoughts even in the presence of others, and this psychological reality has been recognized by modern dramatists whose characters may often be seen thinking to themselves in the most public situations. Whatever the circumstances, private or public, the soliloquy makes unusual demands of both actors and audience.

As readers we should be aware that the soliloquy can perform a variety of functions, and it achieves its purposes with great effectiveness because it is so unusual an element in drama. Customarily, the soliloquy is a means of giving expression to a complex state of mind and feeling, and in most cases the speaker is seen struggling with problems of the utmost consequence. This accounts for the intensity we often find in soliloquys. All of us are familiar, for example, with Hamlet's predicaments—to be or not to be, to kill or not to kill the king—and these are typical of the weighty issues that usually burden the speaker of a soliloquy. Thus in soliloquy the interaction among characters is replaced by the interaction of the mind with itself. To see this element in *Oedipus Rex*, we can turn again to the chorus. No doubt it must seem curious to think of the chorus as soliloquizing—how is it possible, one might

ask, for a group of persons to behave like a single
character in private thought? But it should be noticed
that the chorus is presented collectively as a single
mind, and that its choral odes usually take place when
none of the characters is present. Thus after Oedipus
realizes the full horror of his past and rushes into the
palace to blind himself, the chorus is left alone to seek
its own understanding. And in trying to comprehend
the totality of events, the chorus is clearly meant to
be seen as a single person in the process of meditation
—"Alas for the seed of men. / What measure shall I
give these generations / That breathe on the void and
are void / And exist and do not exist?"

When a play shifts from dramatic interaction to
meditation, the process of events is temporarily sus-
pended, and the soliloquizing character necessarily becomes a spectator of his world. Thus the soliloquy, like
choric commentary, offers the dramatist a means of
providing a point of view on the action of the play.
This goes without saying in the case of the chorus.
But the choric value of soliloquy can also be seen when
Helena, early in the first act of *A Midsummer-Night's
Dream*, reflects on her unrequited love for Demetrius:

> Things base and vile, holding no quantity
> Love can transpose to form and dignity.
> Love looks not with the eyes, but with the mind:
> And therefore is winged Cupid painted blind.
> Nor hath Love's mind of any judgement taste:
> Wings and no eyes figure unheedy haste.

> And therefore is Love said to be a child:
> Because in choice he is so oft beguiled.
> As waggish boys in game themselves forswear:
> So the boy Love is perjured every where.
> For ere Demetrius looked on Hermia's eyne,
> He hailed down oaths that he was only mine.

Helena's personal frustrations unquestionably give rise to these reflections about love, but they are no less valid for having been provoked in this way. And as we see from the subsequent events of the play, Helena's point of view turns out to be extremely accurate. Except for Theseus and Hippolyta, the several lovers *are* "oft beguiled," and "Love *is* perjured every where." Thus in reading soliloquys, we should examine them not only as revelations of character but also as forms of significant commentary on characters and events.

Helena concludes her soliloquy by resolving to inform Demetrius of the meeting in the wood planned by Hermia and Lysander, and the next time we see Helena, in the second act, she is following Demetrius into the wood. This sequence, consisting of Helena's resolve followed later by her joint appearance with Demetrius, points up another important function of the soliloquy. We can call it dramatic economy, for the soliloquized resolve enables Shakespeare to imply rather than show the subsequent action which intervenes. Thus when we see Helena with Demetrius, we can quickly infer that she has been to Athens and provoked his jealous interest in Hermia. The soliloquy, then, by revealing the private resolves of a character becomes an integral part of the action, enabling us to account for an implied sequence of events, and allowing the dramatist to concentrate attention only on the most important elements of the total action.

In considering the soliloquy, we have been looking at an element of meditation in drama. But it is also possible for plays to become primarily or even exclusively meditative. At first thought this probably sounds like a contradiction of dramatic form. If drama depends on the interaction of dialogue, how it is possible for internalized thought and feeling to be the principal subject of a play? Actually, this can happen in a number of ways. Any play which depends heavily on soliloquy, such as Hamlet, tends to take on the qualities of a meditative experience. Proportionally, of course, Hamlet's soliloquys do not represent a very large share of the play. Yet the main action—the revenge plot—depends to a great extent on the working out of Hamlet's private mental processes. Almost everything he does, or does not, do is the result of one soliloquy or the cause of another. And when Hamlet stops soliloquizing, when he turns from private thought to definitive public action, the play comes quickly to an end. Thus in observing Hamlet's behavior, public as well as private, we are witnessing the manifestations of a mind interacting with itself. To this extent *Hamlet* may be seen as an instance of drama moving toward meditation.

But we can also recognize plays, such as *Death of a Salesman* or *A Streetcar Named Desire*, which are almost exclusively concerned with a single consciousness and its interior mental processes. In these plays we encounter not only soliloquys and other kinds of monologue but also imaginary sequences depicting dreams and fantasies. Actually, many modern plays are primarily meditative, because in one way or another they are deeply engaged with psychological theories about the behavior of the mind. If we pause for a moment to look at what a couple of modern dramatists have said about psychology, we can then see its significance for us as readers of modern drama.

Writing in 1932, Eugene O'Neill defined the "modern dramatist's problem" like this:

> . . . how—with the greatest possible dramatic clarity and economy of means—he can express those profound hidden conflicts of the mind which the probings of psychology continue to disclose to us. He must find some method to present this inner drama in his work, or confess himself incapable of portraying one of the most characteristic preoccupations and uniquely significant spiritual impulses of his time.

Almost fifty years before, in 1888, Strindberg was anticipating the same ideas:

> I have noticed that what interests people most nowadays is the psychological action. Our inveterately curious souls are no longer content to see a thing happen;

we want to see how it happens. We want to see the
strings. Look at the machinery, examine the double-
bottom drawer, put on the magic ring to find the
hidden seam, look in the deck for the marked cards.

Looking at these two statements side by side we can
see that they share the same concern. O'Neill speaks
of "inner drama," and Strindberg of "psychological
action." We might also call it meditative drama. In
plays of this kind, interaction among characters is
clearly less important than "hidden conflicts of the
mind." This means that in reading such plays we have
to revise our traditional expectations. Rather than
looking for a plot which clearly has a beginning, mid-
dle, and end, we should expect to find a kind of movement which is as irregular and undefined as the internal
workings of the mind itself. Rather than looking for
things to happen, as in *Oedipus*, *A Midsummer-Night's
Dream*, and the *Misanthrope*, we might expect nothing
to happen, as in *Endgame*, where the game is never
actually concluded.

In a conventional dramatic sense, of course, nothing
does happen in *Endgame*. When the play ends, the
situation of Hamm and Clov is not significantly different from what it was at the beginning. Another day
has passed, bringing Hamm that much closer to his
impending death, but the tension between him and
Clov is unresolved. And the overwhelming condition
of their existence—the deadness of the external uni-

verse—is unchanged. Thus we might very well be moved to say that *Endgame* does not embody a visible plot or action. But it does represent what O'Neill calls an "inner drama"—a psychological action. Considered from this perspective, the plot is made up of the mental activities that Hamm goes through in attempting to deal with his approaching death and the death of the world.

To follow this kind of plot, we have to examine the dialogue with an eye to what it will tell us at any point about Hamm's attitudes and feelings. When he awakes, for example, at the beginning of the play, he asks, "Can there be misery loftier than mine?" This and the statements that follow upon it immediately suggest the histrionic self-pity we come to associate with Hamm. But the self-dramatization, the hamming, quickly yields to a more genuine—and more complicated—response, when he stumbles momentarily into self-awareness:

> Enough, it's time it ended, in the shelter too. (*Pause.*) And yet I hesitate, I hesitate to . . . to end. Yes, there it is, it's time it ended and yet I hesitate to—(*he yawns*)—to end.

Having acknowledged his reluctance "to end," he abruptly tries to distract himself—"God, I'm tired, I'd be better off in bed." So it goes throughout the play, and so it is we must carefully follow the process—the plot —of his psychological behavior.

Up to this point, we have approached the meditative dimension of *Endgame* by taking its characters and their situation at face value, as if they were more or less "realistic" characters in a more or less "realistic" world. But the circumstances of their existence are really extraordinary, so extraordinary in fact as to suggest that they are not merely characters, but that they also represent characteristics—qualities or dimensions of a single mind. The set, for example, consists of a single room with two small windows, one to the left, one to the right, looking out upon the world— like eyeholes. Clov who cannot sit down repeatedly goes to the window to see if anything is taking place outside and reports back to Hamm who is blind and cannot stand up. Clov is obsessed with keeping things neat and in order, while Hamm is the epitome of chaotic and impulsive behavior. Thus it is as if we were looking in upon the interior landscape of a mind and its component qualities—Clov the rational, Hamm the emotional. Hamm, though he is helpless without Clov, exerts a tyrranical control over him. Clov, though he despises Hamm and wishes to leave him, cannot exist apart from him. These tensions account for the main action of the play. Their significance, of course, may be interpreted in various ways, but there can be no doubt that the action shows us a mind for which the world has gone dead, a mind in the process of giving up. Looked at in this way, *Endgame* represents an attempt to reproduce a purely meditative experience in dramatic terms—interaction among characters exists only to represent the interaction of a mind with itself. *Endgame*, then, achieves its "inner drama" through what we might call an allegory of the mind.

Drama cannot get much closer to meditation without relinquishing its essential quality of interaction. For example, in *Krapp's Last Tape*, a play which Beckett wrote shortly after *Endgame*, the only character is Krapp, a sixty-nine-year-old man, and the only action he performs is to listen and react to a tape recording of his voice at the age of thirty-nine. The tape recorder is, admittedly, an ingenious device for creating the sense of another character—Krapp's younger self—and of a dialogue between him and Krapp. But the play is, in fact, a monologue—a meditation—in which Krapp discovers an earlier self so different from his present one that he can no longer identify with his past. Thus *Krapp's Last Tape* exemplifies the point at which drama becomes pure meditation—when it consists exclusively of a single character talking to himself.

Drama and Persuasion. In order for a play to be exclusively a piece of persuasion, it would have to consist of a single character—the dramatist himself—addressing his ideas directly to the audience. But in such an event, it would be difficult to distinguish the play from a lecture. This extreme case should remind us that drama is rarely, if ever, simply an exposition or asser-

tion of ideas. Of course, ideas can be found throughout
the dialogue of almost any play, but as a rule it is best
to assume that those ideas are the sentiments of the
characters, rather than the opinions of the dramatist.
A character is a character. A dramatist is a dramatist.
And the dramatist is never present to speak for himself, except in prefaces, prologues, epilogues, and other
statements outside the framework of the play.

Although the dramatist cannot speak for himself, his
play can. Drama becomes persuasive when its essential
quality is made to serve the purposes of an essay. Thus
a persuasive play uses interaction primarily to expound
ideas and sway the opinions of an audience. In a persuasive play, characters become spokesmen for ideas,
and action becomes an exemplification of ideas. The
desire to persuade usually implies the existence of
conflicting ideas, and persuasive drama customarily
seeks to demonstrate the superiority of one idea, or set
of attitudes, over another. In this respect, a persuasive
play often takes on the qualities of a debate, in which
characters oppose one another and argue their differing
positions. Interaction among characters, therefore, becomes an interplay among conflicting ideas. And plot
is usually the outgrowth of characters putting their
ideas to the test.

As a result of these characteristics, a persuasive play
inevitably forces the audience to examine the merits
of each position and align itself with one side or the

other. Thus in reading a persuasive play, we are usually less interested in the motives and personalities of characters than we are in the ideas they espouse. Similarly, we are less interested in what happens to characters than we are in the success or failure of their ideas. Ultimately, then a persuasive play does not allow us the pleasure of simply witnessing the interaction of characters. Like an essay, it seeks to challenge our ideas and change our minds.

Because it focuses on conflicting ideas, the persuasive play can easily be distinguished from other forms of drama. If we look, for example, at the opening scene of *The Misanthrope*, we can see that it immediately sets up an opposition of values.

PHILINTE When someone greets us with a show of pleasure
          It's but polite to give him equal measure,
          Return his love the best that we know how,
          And trade him offer for offer, vow for vow.

ALCESTE No, no, this formula you'd have me follow
          However fashionable, is false and hollow,
          And I despise the frenzied operations
          Of all these barterers of protestations . . .

PHILINTE But in polite society, custom decrees
          That we show certain outward courtesies. . . .

ALCESTE Ah, no! we should condemn with all our force
          Such false and artificial intercourse.
          Let men behave like men; let them display
          Their inmost hearts in everything they say. . . .

PHILINTE   In certain cases it would be uncouth
           And most absurd to speak the naked truth;
           With all respect for your exalted notion,
           It's often best to veil one's true emotions.

Philinte espouses social propriety, Alceste stands up
for personal integrity, and their disagreement produces
a debate that runs on for more than 150 lines. As
spokesmen for ideas, they behave like contestants in a
formal argument, rather than characters in a dramatic
situation. And their dialogue sounds like disputation
rather than conversation. Philinte's initial proposition
is countered by Alceste's denial; Alceste's denial is
answered by Philinte's rebuttal; Philinte's rebuttal is re-
jected by Alceste's assertion; Alceste's assertion is
attacked by Philinte's counterassertion; and so on, and
so on. The formal pattern of debate, echoed here by
the formal rhythm of couplet verse, sharpens our
awareness of the conflicting ideas. By the end of this
scene, then, the play has clearly invited us to take a
stand, to choose between "ourward courtesies" and
"inmost hearts." The choice, of course, is not an easy
one, and the play is designed to keep us from making
a simple decision.

PART TWO

MODES OF DRAMA

I DRAMA, THE WORLD, AND IMITATION

. . . suit the action to the word, the word to the action;
with this special observance, that you o'erstep not the
modesty of nature: for anything so overdone is from the
purpose of playing, whose end, both at the first and now,
was and is, to hold, as 'twere, the mirror up to nature; to
show virtue her own feature, scorn her own image, and
the very age and body of the time his form and pressure.

So Hamlet advises the Players. And his advice should
serve to remind us that the literary and theatrical elements of drama, the words and actions, cannot be considered apart from their purpose—"to hold, as't were,
the mirror up to nature." Drama, as we said in the
beginning, creates a world modelled on our own. Its
essence is imitative action.

But drama is not imitative in the ordinary sense of
the word. It does not offer us a literal copy of reality,
for the truth of drama does not depend on reproducing
the world exactly as it is. Drama is true to life by being

41

false to our conventional notions of reality. The behavior of Alceste is outlandish. The story of Oedipus
is highly improbable. The predicament of Hamm and
Clov is absurd. And the events of *A Midsummer-
Night's Dream* are fantastic. Yet each of these plays
creates a world that we recognize as being in some
sense like our own. Our problem, then, is to define the
precise sense in which drama is imitative.

If we return to Hamlet's remarks, we can find a solu-
tion to the problem. When Hamlet explains what he
means by holding "the mirror up to nature," it becomes clear that he has in mind an extraordinary kind
of mirror—a mirror which is able to reflect the essence
of things, "to show virtue her own feature, scorn her
own image." Drama is like such a mirror because its
mode of imitation is selective and intensive. And it has
to be. In the theater time is short and space is limited.
Faced with limitations in stage size and performance
time, the dramatist obviously cannot hope to reproduce
the world as it is. But by selecting and intensifying
things, he can emphasize the dominant patterns and
essential qualities of human experience. Thus our understanding of any play requires that we define the
principle of emphasis that determines the make-up of
its world and the experience of its characters.

II MODES OF IMITATION: ROMANCE AND SATIRE;
COMEDY AND TRAGEDY

In defining the emphasis of any play, we can begin by
asking ourselves whether the dramatist in holding up
his mirror has focused on the beautiful or the ugly, on
the orderly or the chaotic, on what is best or what is
worst in the world. A play that emphasizes the beautiful and the orderly tends toward an idealized vision of
the world, which is the mode we call romance. A play
that focuses on the ugly and chaotic tends toward a
debased view of the world, and this we call satire.
Since both of these emphases depend for their effect
upon extreme views of human existence, the characters
who populate romance and satire rarely undergo any
change. The idealized figure is ideal because he does
not change and cannot be changed. The same is true
of the debased character.

In contrast to the relatively static conditions of
romance and satire, we can observe a pair of dynamic
processes which take place in a world neither so beautiful as that of romance, nor so ugly as that of satire—in
a world more nearly like our own. Rather than focus-
ing on essential qualities in the world, these processes
—comedy and tragedy—emphasize the dominant patterns of experience that characters undergo in the
world. In comedy, the principal characters ordinarily
begin in a state of opposition either to one another or

their world—often both. By the end of the play, their
opposition is replaced by harmony. Thus the characters
are integrated with one another and with their world.
In tragedy, however, the hero and his world begin in
a condition of harmony which disintegrates, leaving
him, by the end of the play, in a state of isolation.

With these four possibilities in mind, we can draw
a simple diagram, like this:

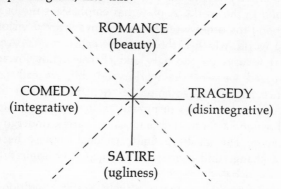

The vertical pair emphasize the essential qualities in
the world; the horizontal pair emphasize the dominant
patterns of human experience. Thus the point of inter-
section, the absence of emphasis, refers to the world
as it is. In this way, we can immediately visualize each
of the emphases, its distinguishing characteristics, and
its relation to one another.

Once we have recognized these possibilities, our
natural inclination is to categorize and analyze plays

in terms of the characteristics we have identified with each emphasis. But it should be kept in mind that each of these emphases is at best an abstraction—a definition formulated in order to generalize about a great number of plays, not an explanation of any single play in particular. Thus when we turn to individual plays, we should not necessarily expect that they can be accurately described and understood simply by labeling them comedy or tragedy, satire or romance. As a way of anticipating some of the complexities, we can look at the diagram and see that although each emphasis occurs within carefully defined limits, it also borders on two others. Comedy, for example, tends toward romance, on the one hand, and satire on the other. The same is true of tragedy. And so on. Even the antithetical possibilities, as we will see, can interact with one another. But this should hardly surprise us. If the world can incorporate both the beautiful and the ugly, so can a play.

III   DRAMATIC MODES IN "THE MISANTHROPE,"
      "A MIDSUMMER-NIGHT'S DREAM," "ENDGAME,"
      AND "OEDIPUS REX"

The Misanthrope is a clear-cut example of how a single play can incorporate more than one principle of emphasis. A survey of the characters immediately tells us that we are in the world of satire, for this is a play filled with ugly people. Célimène is a flighty and malicious coquette, Arsinoé a jealous and hypocritical prude, Oronte a vain poet and officious lover, Acaste and Clitandre a matched pair of pretentious fops. Even Alceste, the self-proclaimed honest man, the moral scourge of his society, is badly flawed by his extraordinary egotism. Thus the world of these characters strikes us as unrelievedly false and shallow. And as we might expect in satire, the characters do not undergo any change. Alceste's histrionic misanthropy persists to the very end, even though it costs him the hand of Célimène.

On the basis of this evidence, it would be inappropriate to think of *The Misanthrope* as a comedy. But it does contain a dimension we associate with comedy, and surprisingly an element from the world of romance. Up to this point we have not mentioned Philinte and Éliante, primarily, of course, because they do not belong to the satiric landscape we have observed in the play. Yet they cannot be ignored, for they are essential to the view of the world that Molière offers us. Philinte, though he perceives the hypocrisy of society as clearly as Alceste, is able to control his temper through a philosophic acceptance of things. Occasionally he is a bit too willing to "forget the follies of the times / And pardon mankind for its petty crimes." Even so, he embodies the views of the reasonable man. In this respect he is the antithesis of Alceste. To an even greater degree Éliante is the antithesis of Célimène. When Célimène gossips, Éliante is silent. While Célimène encourages innumerable suitors, Éliante devotes herself unselfishly to Alceste. She is, in fact, a flawless character, an idealized figure, from the world of romance. Her presence in the play, like that of Philinte, need not baffle us, however. The beauty of her character only serves to make us more painfully aware of the ugliness that surrounds her. Similarly, her marriage to Philinte, the harmonious resolution we expect from comedy, poignantly emphasizes the continued opposition between Alceste and Célimène.

A Midsummer-Night's Dream also brings together several emphases, but it does so in a different way with different effects from *The Misanthrope*. The cast of characters alone is enough to show us that Shakespeare has not focused on a single dimension of reality. At one extreme we have Oberon, Titania, and the world of fairies. At the other, Quince, Bottom, and the "mechanicals." In between, we have the court world of Theseus and Hippolyta, as well as the distinctly different realm of the four lovers. Clearly, it would be inaccurate to describe the play in terms of a single emphasis. Oberon and Titania, for example, though extremely beautiful creatures whom we might want to regard as romance figures, belong to the world of fantasy. Furthermore, they are so badly afflicted by the fickleness of their desires that it would be inappropriate to associate them with the flawless world of romance.

Theseus and Hippolyta, as we see them in the play, might qualify as romance figures. Their love is constant, their behavior dignified, their court the one source of order in the play. But our perception of their excellence is modified by what we know of their wanton pasts. The four young lovers obviously do not belong to romance, nor for that matter to satire. Though afflicted by the problems of love, many of the problems are clearly not of their own making. They belong to a world most nearly like our own. Bottom and his friends show signs of a satiric emphasis. Thus their clumsy rehearsals, their fumbling performance, and the grotesque image of Bottom equipped with the head of an ass. Yet we obviously are not meant to think of them in the same terms as the characters from the satiric world of *The Misanthrope*. Bottom and his friends are, after all, merely harmless fools, whose theatrical bumbling makes farcical fare of a tragic love story. Thus we respond to their flaws, as does Theseus, with tolerant amusement rather than disgust. Ultimately, then, the world of *A Midsummer-Night's Dream* encompasses a wide range of possibilities moving from the mildly satiric through romance to fantasy. But this should not cause us problems in understanding, for we can see that in each of the levels Shakespeare in one way or another is dramatizing his theme —the irrational nature of love.

Shifting our attention from the characters to the plot of *A Midsummer-Night's Dream*, we can finally

identify the main emphasis of the play. The play begins with the principal characters, the young lovers, in
a state of opposition to one another and to their world.
Helena loves Demetrius. But Demetrius loves and has
the consent to marry Hermia. But Hermia loves Lysander. And though Lysander also loves Hermia, her
father Egeus refuses to sanction their marriage. The
complications of the young lovers are mirrored in the
jealous opposition of Oberon and Titania. But through
the whimsical agency of Puck, the lovers are finally
paired off, Oberon and Titania are reconciled, and the
play ends in the harmonious integration typical of
comedy. Marriages abound, and nothing is allowed to
shatter that harmony, not even the tragic love story of
Pyramus and Thisbe.

By comparison with *The Misanthrope* and *A Midsummer-Night's Dream*, the emphasis of *Endgame* may
appear simple to identify and understand. The world
of Hamm and Clov is unspeakably ugly and chaotic.
Our first and enduring image of Hamm—"a stiff toque
on his head, a large blood-stained handkerchief over his
face, a whistle hanging from his head"—seems evidence enough to assure us that we have entered a
grimly satiric world. And everything that we see in
the play confirms this first impression—from the com-
pulsive chatter and busyness of Clov, to the ashbin
containing the senile and starving parents of Hamm.
Things are so bad off in this world that even nature
seems to have gone dead—rain never comes and the

sun never shines. Certainly, then, there can be no
question about Beckett's intention to emphasize through
this dark vision the loneliness, the meaninglessness,
the unremitting pain of existence. But if we stop here,
we will fail to see the complexity with which Beckett
develops this view of things.

Although the play is clearly located in the world of
satire, it has certain qualities that we tend to associate
with either comedy or tragedy. The play opens in a
state of tension, of opposition, between Hamm and
Clov—Clov threatening to leave Hamm, Hamm rebuk-
ing Clov for his cruelty. And in their early dialogue,
they sound like a pair of quarreling lovers:

> HAMM You're leaving me all the same
> CLOV I'm trying.
> HAMM You don't love me.
> CLOV No.
> HAMM You loved me once.
> CLOV Once!
> HAMM I've made you suffer too much.

Thus they seem wedded to one another as uncomfort-
ably as ham and cloves. As a result, the play immediately sets up the kind of situation we might associate
with comedy, and we look forward to a definitive resolution of their predicament. In the same way, we—
and they—wonder whether the world outside will
come alive. But the action of the play repeatedly frus-
trates us—and them. At the end Clov is standing by

the door "impassive and motionless." The endgame results in a stalemate. Their situation is unresolved one way or the other. In much the same fashion, the play embodies certain tragic potentialities. Hamm is clearly to be seen as a heroic figure in his world. Throughout the play, he is seated squarely in the center of the stage, as if to suggest his kingly role. And if we can believe Hamm's story of his life, he was in the pre-play action a figure of similar authority. Having acknowledged the catastrophe in the external universe, Hamm awaits with eagerness the disintegration of his own. But as we know, the action of the play denies him that dignity and certitude. Thus *Endgame* is neither comedy nor tragedy, neither integration nor disintegration. And in being neither one nor the other, it is process without purpose. In this way, the comic and tragic potentialities reinforce the satiric emphasis of the play.

In contrast to *Endgame*, as well as the other plays we have looked at, *Oedipus Rex* is designed in terms of one emphasis and one emphasis only. It is tragedy pure and simple. Nothing impedes the unremitting movement that carries Oedipus from king to outcast. Nothing distracts our attention—or his—from the inquiry that discovers the infamy of Oedipus at the same time that it discloses the identity of the criminal. Thus everything works to emphasize the pattern of disintegration. The Priest, Creon, Teiresias, Jocasta, the Messenger, the Shepherd, and the Second Messenger—

each in his turn marks a distinct stage in the process that begins with the dignity of Oedipus and ends in his undoing. To the Priest in the beginning, he is "powerful King," "wisest in the ways of God," "Noblest of Men," "Liberator." His harmony with the world and his mastery of it are unquestioned. But to the Second Messenger at the end, he is a figure of "ruin" and "disgrace."

The character of Oedipus is perfectly consistent with the experience he undergoes. His dignity is manifest not only in his title but also in his action. He is unrelenting in his quest for truth. Even when the search for the criminal suddenly turns into an investigation of his own identity, he does not cease. Even though Teiresias warns him and Jocasta seeks to dissuade him, he refuses to give in. Thus his relentless devotion to truth becomes the source of both his glory and his ruin. For he discovers the truth, and in doing so he cures the city even as he exposes his own sickness. His pride, therefore, is of a very special kind. It is a pride born of an extraordinary mind. The process of reasoning that led him to flee from Corinth, to murder Laios, to solve the riddle of the Sphinx, to discover the criminal and his own identity—this process enabled him to master his universe, or at least one dimension of it. And his self-imposed blindness speaks for his recognition of a world within and beyond not to be mastered by any act of mind. In this sense, the experience of

Oedipus, which is the experience of pure tragedy,
authenticates both the dignity and the frailty of man.

> Men of Thebes: look upon Oedipus
> This is the king who solved the riddle
> And towered up, most powerful of men.
> No mortal eyes but looked on him with envy,
> Yet in the end ruin swept over him.
>
> Let every man in mankind's frailty
> Consider his last day; and let none
> Presume on his good fortune until he find
> Life, at his death, a memory without pain.

PART THREE

ELEMENTS OF DRAMA

Character, dialogue, plot. These are the indispensable elements of drama. Together they make possible the imitative world of every play, for characters are like people, dialogue and plot like the things they say and do. But likeness does not mean identicalness. As we indicated in our discussion of dramatic modes, the truth of drama does not depend upon reproducing the world exactly as it is. Thus in examining the elements of a play, we should not expect to find characters who talk and act in just the same way that people do. And we should not expect to find plots that develop in just the same way that ordinary events do. The characters who populate romance and satire, for example, are modeled less on people than on human potentialities. Similarly, the plots that take place in comedy and tragedy are based less on real occurrences than on basic patterns of human experience. The elements of drama, then, are highly specialized versions of the elements that make up the world as it is. The particular versions we encounter in any single play will be determined by a number of circumstances. Clearly enough, dramatic modes have a good deal to do with producing one kind of character rather than another, or one kind of plot rather than another. Equally important are the contexts of drama we discussed in the first section of our study. Obviously, the characters, dialogue, and plot of an essayistic play are bound to be quite different from those of a meditative play. And the elements of a play conceived for the classical Greek stage are bound to take a different form from the elements of a play conceived for the Renaissance English theater. Therefore, when we study the elements of drama, we should remember that they are to a great extent determined by the contexts and modes of drama.

II   DIALOGUE

The give and take of dialogue is a highly specialized form of conversation. Designed to serve the needs created by the various contexts and modes of drama, it can hardly be expected to sound like our customary patterns of speech. In ordinary conversation, for example, we adjust our style to meet the needs of the people with whom we are talking, and we reinforce our words with a wide range of facial expressions, bodily gestures, and vocal inflections, many of which we perform quite unconsciously. If we recognize that we are not being understood, we may stammer momentarily, while we try to rephrase our feelings and ideas. But before we can get the words out, someone may have interrupted us, completely changing the topic of conversation. Whatever the case, we continually find ourselves rapidly adjusting to circumstances that are as random as our own thoughts and the thoughts of those with whom we are talking. Thus if we were to transcribe and then listen to the tape of an ordinary conversation, even one which we considered to be coherent and orderly, we would probably find it far more erratic and incoherent than we had imagined.

Drama cannot afford to reproduce conversation as faithfully as a tape recorder. To begin with, the limitations of performance time require that characters express their ideas and feelings much more economically than we do in the leisurely course of ordinary conversation. The conditions of theatrical performance also demand that dialogue be formulated not only so that it can be heard by characters talking to one another on stage, but also so that it can be overheard and understood by the audience in the theater. Consequently, the continuity of dialogue must be very clearly marked out at every point. On the basis of what it overhears, the audience—or the reader—must be able to infer the nature of each character, the public and private relationships among the several characters, the past as well as the present circumstances in which the various char-

acters are involved. Dialogue, then, is an extraordinarily significant form of conversation, for it is the means
by which every play implies the total make-up of its
imaginative world. And this is not all. Dialogue must
fulfill the needs of not only the audience but also the
actors; it is the script from which the actors take their
cues. This means that dialogue must imply the whole
range of expressions, gestures, inflections, and movements required in performance.

Because it has to serve so many purposes all at once,
dialogue is necessarily a much more artificial form of
discourse than ordinary conversation. Thus in reading
any segment of dialogue, we should always keep in
mind its numerous purposes. Here, for example, is a
passage from the end of Act I, scene i, of *The Misanthrope*. Read it through and see what you can infer on
your own before turning to the commentary that fol-
lows.

PHILINTE   . . .
Rage less at your opponent, and give some thought
To how you'll win this lawsuit that he's brought.
ALCESTE   I assure you I'll do nothing of the sort.
PHILINTE   Then who will plead your case before the court?
ALCESTE   Reason and right and justice will plead for me.
PHILINTE   Oh, Lord. What judges do you plan to see?
ALCESTE   Why, none. The justice of my cause is clear.
PHILINTE   Of course, man; but there's politics to fear. . . .
ALCESTE   No, I refuse to lift a hand. That's flat.
I'm either right, or wrong.

PHILINTE   Don't count on that.

ALCESTE   No, I'll do nothing.

PHILINTE   Your enemy's influence
Is great, you know . . .

ALCESTE   That makes no difference.

PHILINTE   It will; you'll see.

ALCESTE   Must honor bow to guile?
If so, I shall be proud to lose the trial.

PHILINTE   Oh, really . . .

ALCESTE   I'll discover by this case
Whether or not men are sufficiently base
And impudent and villainous and perverse
To do me wrong before the universe.

PHILINTE   What a man!

ALCESTE   Oh, I could wish, whatever the cost,
Just for the beauty of it, that my trial were lost.

PHILINTE   If people heard you talking so, Alceste,
They'd split their sides. Your name would be a jest.

ALCESTE   So much the worse for jesters.

PHILINTE   May I enquire
Whether this rectitude you so admire,
And these hard virtues you're enamored of
Are qualities of the lady whom you love?
It much surprises me that you, who seem
To view mankind with furious disesteem,
Have yet found something to enchant your eyes
Amidst a species which you so despise.
And what is more amazing, I'm afraid,
Is the most curious choice your heart has made.
The honest Eliante is fond of you,

Arsinoe, the prude, admires you too;
And yet your spirit's been perversely led
To choose the flighty Celimene instead,
Whose brittle malice and coquettish ways
So typify the manners of our days.
How is it that the traits you most abhor
Are bearable in this lady you adore?
Are you so blind with love that you can't find
    them?
Or do you contrive, in her case, not to mind them?

ALCESTE   My love for that young widow's not the kind
That can't perceive defects; no, I'm not blind.
I see her faults, despite my ardent love,
And all I see I fervently reprove.
And yet I'm weak; for all her falsity,
That woman knows the art of pleasing me,
And though I never cease complaining of her,
I swear I cannot manage not to love her.
Her charm outweights her faults; I can but aim
To cleanse her spirit in my love's pure flame.

PHILINIE   That's no small task; I wish you all success.
You think then that she loves you?

ALCESTE   Heavens, yes!
I wouldn't love her did she not love me.

PHILINTE   Well, if her taste for you is plain to see,
Why do these rivals cause you such despair?

ALCESTE   True love, Sir, is possessive, and cannot bear
To share with all the world. I'm here today
To tell her she must send that mob away.

PHILINTE   If I were you, and had your choice to make,
Eliante, her cousin, would be the one I'd take;

> That honest heart, which cares for you alone,
> Would harmonize far better with your own.
>
> ALCESTE   True, true: each day my reason tells me so;
> But reason doesn't rule in love, you know.
>
> PHILINTE   I fear some bitter sorrow is in store;
> This love . . .

To begin with, we should notice that Alceste and Philinte speak in rhymed couplets. This may strike us at first as being unusually artificial, but the artificiality is perfectly in keeping with the sophisticated manners of a high society such as Molière depicts in the play. Thus the elegance and intelligence of the characters are intensified by their well-turned couplets. Furthermore, as we observed earlier, the couplets heighten our awareness of the conflicting positions in the argument between Alceste and Philinte. Notice, for example, that in the opening part of the passage Alceste and Philinte reply to one another in single lines which combine to produce a series of couplets. Yet in each instance, Philinte completes the couplet that Alceste has begun. This tends to create the impression that Philinte repeatedly has the last word in the argument. Following this rapid give and take, Philinte suddenly launches into an extended speech culminating in a series of pointed questions. In this way he abruptly changes the pace of the discussion and puts Alceste in a defensive position. At this point, we might observe that the conversation breaks into two distinct parts— the first concerned with Alceste's lawsuit, the second with his love affair. And the change in topic occurs simultaneously with the change in pace. Thus the form of the dialogue serves to mark out the important points of its continuity.

If we return again to the beginning of the conversation and examine it somewhat more closely, we can see how the character of each man is implied by the form and content of his statements. Philinte, for example, assumes the role of a pragmatic adviser, continually reminding Alceste of the ins and outs of law courts— "who will plead your case," "what judges do you plan to see," "there's politics to fear," "your enemy's influence is great." Alceste, on the other hand, sounds like a fearless moral idealist—"Reason and right and justice will plead for me," "The justice of my case is clear," "I'm either right or wrong." If we try to imagine how their lines would sound in performance, we can easily hear a difference in tone which suggests that Philinte is a far more gracious and amiable character than Alceste, whose inflexibility makes him appear somewhat boorish by comparison. It must be acknowledged, of course, that Alceste's defiant tone is morally admirable, far more so than Philinte's prudently lawyerish manner. But as the dialogue progresses, we can detect another side to Alceste's moral stand which undercuts the purity of his convictions. When he says, for example, "Must honor bow to guile? / If so, I shall be proud to lose the trial," we notice that Alceste seems to indulge his vanity by viewing defeat as if it were a form of martyrdom. And when a few lines later, he exclaims that "I could wish, whatever the cost, / Just for the beauty of it, that my trial were lost," he confirms our suspicion that his behavior is motivated as much by egotism as by moral integrity. Thus when Philinte strategically shifts the topic of conversation, and asks if "these hard virtues you're enamored of / Are qualities of the lady whom you love," we are forced to recognize yet another inconsistency in the moral posturing of Alceste. Obviously his passions are not in keeping with his principles—except for the fact that they also seem to be complicated by his irrepressible egotism.

In addition to revealing the character of Philinte and Alceste, this passage also provides us with significant information about the qualities of their world and the other persons who inhabit it. The discussion of Alceste's lawsuit reveals a legal system corrupted by "politics" and "influence." The discussion of Alceste's love affairs reveals a social mode dominated by "brittle malice and coquettish ways." And about these conditions both of the men agree. Thus we have no reason to believe otherwise. They also agree about the honesty of Éliante and the falsity of Célimène. If we are listening closely, we will also be alert to Philinte's special admiration for Éliante, and the way in which he expresses it:

If I were you, and had your choice to make
Éliante, her cousin, would be the one I'd take

Thus we should not be totally surprised when Philinte proposes to Éliante at the end of the play.

Although our discussion of this passage has gone on far longer than the passage itself, we have by no means commented fully on its significance. We might, for example, have gone into what it tells us about the rivalries of the several men and women in the play, preparing us for later developments in the plot. But we have gone far enough in our analysis to see how many different purposes can be carried out within a relatively brief segment of dialogue. Thus in reading dialogue, we should continually be alert to everything it can tell us about the character who is speaking, the character who is listening, the other characters who are not present, the relationships among the characters, the quality of the world they inhabit, the circumstances that cause their interaction with one another, the events that are likely to follow from their interaction, and so on.

III   PLOT

Plot is a highly specialized form of experience. We can see just how specialized it is if we consider for a moment what happens during the ordinary course of our experience. Between waking and sleeping, we

probably converse with a number of people and perform a variety of actions. But most of these events
have very little to do with one another, and they
usually serve no purpose other than our pleasure, our
work, or our bodily necessities. Thus the events that
take place in our daily existence do not embody a
significant pattern or process. If they have any pattern
at all, it is merely the product of habit and routine.

But in drama, every event is part of a carefully
designed pattern and process. And this is what we call
plot. Plot, then, is not at all like the routine, and often
random, course of our daily existence. It is, instead, a
wholly interconnected system of events, deliberately
selected and arranged, in order to fulfill a complex set
of dramatic purposes and theatrical conditions. Thus
plot is an extremely artificial element, and it has to be.
In the period of a few hours, the interest of spectators
has to be deeply engaged and continuously sustained.
Their interest must be aroused by events that make up
a process capable of being represented on stage. And
the totality of events must create a coherent imitation
of the world.

In order to understand how plot fulfills these multiple purposes, we should begin by recognizing that it
comprises *everything* which takes place in the imaginative world of a play. This means that plot is not confined merely to what takes place on stage. Plot includes
reported, as well as represented, action. In *Oedipus
Rex*, for example, we witness what might be called a

process of criminal investigation, in which the investigator discovers himself to be the criminal and inflicts the appropriate punishment for his crime. But we do not witness all of the events that make up that process and contribute to its development. The wisdom of the Oracle is reported by Creon, the death of Polybus is reported by the First Messenger, the suicide of Jocasta and the self-blinding of Oedipus are reported by the Second Messenger. Obviously, all of these events take place in the imaginative world of the play. They are part of the plot. But they are not part of what we call the scenario—the action that takes place on stage. Similarly, in *The Misanthrope*, we witness a process which includes among other events a lawsuit brought against Alceste, tried in court, and judged in favor of his enemy. Yet we never actually see his enemy, nor do we hear the case being tried. We only hear *about* it from the dialogue of Alceste and Philinte. Thus if we wish to identify the plot of a play, we will have to distinguish it from the scenario. The scenario embodies the plot and interprets it for us, but it is not the same things as the plot.

We can recognize this distinction in another way if we consider the order in which events may be presented to us in a play. In *Oedipus Rex*, for example, the death of Polybus takes place before the time of the action on stage. Similarly, in *The Misanthrope*, the lawsuit is brought against Alceste before the opening discussion between him and Philinte. But in both cases these events are reported to us only after the stage action is well under way. In the plot, of course, these events are linked to one another by an unalterable chronology. But in the scenario, these same events have been presented to us in an entirely different order. Thus in studying the plot of a play, we must examine not only the events of which it consists, but also the complex ways in which those events are presented by the scenario.

As an example of the analytic procedure this requires, we might look at *A Midsummer-Night's Dream*. To begin with we should note that the plot, unlike that of *Oedipus Rex*, combines several lines of interest and distinct groupings of characters. The marriage plans of Theseus and Hippolyta constitute one line of interest. The entangled love affairs of Demetrius, Lysander, Hermia, and Helena constitute a second story line. The theatrical ventures of the "hempen homespuns" constitute a third line of action. And the love conflicts of Titania and Oberon constitute a fourth line of interest. The first three of these story lines are introduced in the first act of the play. During the next three acts, all four of the lines converge in the forest, and characters from each line interact with one another. In the final act, we witness the festivities at court that take place once the confusions and tensions in each story line have been resolved. This much is clear from a quick survey of the plot. But the energy and excitement of the play are produced by the way these elements of the plot are put together and presented in the scenario.

If we look more closely at the first act, we can see how these elements are selected and arranged to manipulate our perception and experience of the plot. In order to do this, it is best to think of the act as being made up of a series of dramatic units—each time a character enters or leaves the stage a new dramatic unit begins. Thus the appearance or departure of a character or group of characters is like a form of punctuation that we should take special note of whenever we are reading or witnessing a play. As one grouping of characters yields to another, the dramatic situation changes, sometimes slightly, sometimes very perceptibly, carrying the play forward in the development of its process and the fulfillment of its plot.

The act begins with a brief dramatic unit involving Theseus, Hippolyta, Philostrate, and attendants. The dialogue between Theseus and Hippolyta expresses their shared anticipation of the "nuptial hour" and concludes with Theseus directing Philostrate to "stir up the Athenian youths to merriments." Thus the opening unit immediately establishes a comic mood of celebration that we associate with an impending marriage. And the departure of Philostrate invites us to speculate about the festivities to come. After Philostrate has departed, Theseus in the next unit continues to sound the festive tone, telling Hippolyta that he will wed her "with pomp, with triumph, and with revelling." At this point, the plot seems to have no source of complication, and nowhere to go—marriage, after all, is the ritual of harmony we expect at the end of comedy, not at the beginning. But the complication is not long in coming.

In the next dramatic unit, marked by the entrance of Egeus, Hermia, Lysander, and Demetrius, the tangled affairs of the young lovers are extensively dramatized. In his lengthy address to Theseus, Egeus begins by announcing the marriage he has approved between Demetrius and Hermia, then he launches into an extended complaint against Lysander whom he claims has "filched my daughter's heart." In the remainder of the unit, Hermia and Lysander plead their case, but Egeus is unyielding, and Theseus rules that Hermia must obey her father's will or submit to the law of Athens. Thus at the end of this unit, marked by the departure of everyone but Hermia and Lysander, a major complication in the plot has been established, and our interest is aroused in how it will be resolved.

In addition to noting how this sequence of units prepares for the development of the plot, we should also consider how the arrangement of dramatic units shapes our understanding of the plot. By doing so, we can see that the juxtaposition of this lengthy unit with the two brief ones immediately preceding it creates a number of important effects. To begin with, the recurrence of marriage as the focus of interest in each unit suggests that it will probably be an element of major thematic importance in the play. Consequently, we are moved to contrast the heroic love of Theseus and Hippolyta, the romantic love of Lysander and Hermia, and the fickle love of Demetrius for Hermia. Finally, the comparative length of the three units, suggests that the attention of the play will be focused on the entanglements of the young lovers and that the impending marriage of Theseus and Hippolyta will serve primarily as a frame surrounding other lines of interest.

These assumptions are confirmed by the next dramatic unit involving Hermia and Lysander, who spend the first part of their dialogue lamenting that "the course of true love never did run smooth." In the second part of the unit they agree to meet in the forest, flee Athens, and be married elsewhere. Thus by the end of this unit, marked with the appearance of Helena, we are more deeply involved in the meaning and process of the action concerning the young lovers. This focus is continued in the next unit, which complicates the plot by revealing Helena's frustrated love for Demetrius. Helena, of course, is distressed by Demetrius' love of Hermia, whereupon Hermia and Lysander disclose their secret marriage plans in order to assure Helena that at least one obstacle to her love will be removed. The unit ends with the departure of Hermia and Lysander, leaving Helena alone to soliloquize about the fickleness of love. We have already discussed her soliloquy in the section on drama and meditation (see pp. 30-32), but we can now see from our study of plot that the soliloquy gains additional power and significance from its special location in the scenario. Coming as it does at the end of a lengthy series of units which focus on the plight of the young lovers, Helena's meditation intensifies our perception of their experience by viewing it in terms of the myth of Cupid and the abstract nature of love. Thus her soliloquy offers a perspective for understanding not only the events that have just taken place at court, but also the developments we look forward to witnessing in the forest.

By this point in the play, we may be so involved in the complicated situation of the young lovers that we have forgotten the marriage festivities being planned for Theseus and Hippolyta. Thus the next unit marked by the departure of Helena and the appearance of Quince, Bottom, and the other "mechanicals" reminds us of the opening unit when Theseus ordered Philostrate to "awake the pert and nimble spirit of mirth." By recalling the earlier unit, we can also see an example of how the scenario implies events in the plot without having to represent them on stage. Following his departure, Philostrate must have announced the festivities throughout Athens, and Quince hearing the announcement must have gathered his actors together to rehearse their play. Yet, all of this activity is implied simply by the command of Theseus, the departure of Philostrate, and the opening line of Quince, "Is all our company here?" Every dramatist uses this kind of shorthand to extend the activity of his

imaginative world beyond the physical limits of the
stage. This aspect of plot is what we call implied action, and in reading or witnessing a play we should
always be alert to indications of it in the scenario.

Quince and his fellows spend the entire unit comi-
cally fumbling with the theatrical problems of casting
and staging their play. Thus the tone and action of this
unit provide a dramatic contrast to the serious business
of the immediately preceding units. Despite this contrast, the units are related to one another in a very
important way. The "mechanicals" plan to produce a
play based on the tragic love story of Pyramus and
Thisbe, and in several respects this story is quite similar to the predicament of the four young lovers. But as
we witness the rehearsal, it becomes clear that the tragedy will be transformed to farce by this ludicrously inept
group of actors. In fact, Quince calls their play "The
most lamentable comedy and most cruel death of Pyramus and Thisbe." If we are alert to the context and
implications of this incongruous remark, we can see
that it offers another perspective on the young lovers,
and the problems of romantic love. Clearly, we are not
meant to take the love problems too seriously. If anything, the comic rehearsal of a tragic love story reminds
us that what we have been witnessing is also a play—
an imaginative situation contrived for our amusement.
The unit ends with Quince requesting his fellows to
meet the following night in the forest—the same place
where Hermia and Lysander have agreed to meet, and

the same place where Helena hopes to lure Demetrius. Thus if we have been paying attention to the earlier details, we can easily anticipate an elaborate sequence of events in the woods. And this supposition is immediately confirmed by the next unit which opens the second act with Puck and a Fairy talking about the conflict between Oberon and Titania, as well as the revels they have planned in the forest.

If we continued with our analysis, we would have to answer a number of questions about the unit involving Puck and the Fairy. What effects are produced by juxtaposing the dialogue of the Fairies and the rehearsal of the mechanicals? How does their dialogue modify our previous expectations about the plot? How does it prepare for future developments in the plot? In what ways does their discussion of Oberon and Titania relate to the love theme of the play? How does this unit affect our perception of the imaginative world embodied in the play?

On the basis of these questions and our discussion of the first act, it should be obvious that plot is an extremely complicated element that can only be understood through a painstaking analysis of dramatic units. Here are some reminders and suggestions to follow in analyzing the plot of any play. Identify *all* the events that take place during the plot and the chronological order in which they occur. In order to do this, examine the scenario in detail, paying careful attention to instances of implied and reported action. Determine

whether the plot is simple or complex, whether it consists of a single line of action or multiple lines of
action. If the plot is simple, define the sequence of
cause and effect that leads from one event to the next.
If the plot is complex, identify each line of action and
the points at which they interact with one another.
Once the details and make-up of the plot have been
established, then examine the way in which the plot is
presented by the scenario. In order to do this, analyze
each dramatic unit in detail, beginning with the first
and proceeding consecutively throughout the play.
Remember that a single dramatic unit can serve a
variety of purposes. Remember too that every unit
exists within a context of units.

IV CHARACTER

Characters in a play are not the same as people in real
life. To think otherwise is tempting, but we should
never ignore the fact that characters exist in an imaginative world. Real people live in the world as it is.
Biological, psychological, and social conditions affect
the behavior of real people. Dramatic and theatrical
necessities determine the nature of characters. Thus
characters are like real people in some respects, but in
other respects they are not like real people at all.

We can see how these differences arise by recalling
the contexts, modes, and other elements of drama. In

the classical Greek theater, for example, characters were visually defined by the fixed expressions of their facial masks. Clearly, it would have been impossible to respond to these characters as if they were complex human personalities. And if we look at Oedipus, we can see that he is conceived in terms of only a few dominant traits—traits that could be projected through the bold style of acting required by the size and shape of the Greek theater.

Even when theatrical conditions allow for greater psychological detail, there are usually other dramatic circumstances that work against the formation of completely lifelike characters. In *A Midsummer-Night's Dream*, for example, plot is obviously a much more important element than character. In fact, the characters in this play are conceived primarily to suit the needs of the plot. Thus Egeus exists only to create an obstacle to the love of Lysander and Hermia. If we try to plumb the depths of his personality, we will probably find that he is motivated exclusively by his sense of paternal authority, which makes it possible for him to create the obstacle required by a comic plot. Similarly, if we try to distinguish Demetrius from Lysander, we will probably find only a few minor differences, for their similarity is necessary in order to make possible the multiple confusions in the forest.

In *The Misanthrope*, plot is less important than character, but character is less important than the essayistic form and satiric mode of the play. Thus as we have seen, Alceste and Philinte have personality traits consistent with the ideas they espouse. And the other characters, such as Acaste and Clitandre, or Arsinoé and Célimène, are exaggerated versions of objectionable human tendencies that show up in high society. They are character types consistent with Molière's satiric purpose.

Because of its recurrent interest in psychological behavior, modern drama tends to put a great deal of emphasis on character. But even plays, such as *Endgame*, which are specifically concerned with the inner workings of the human mind, do not embody characters who can be taken as identical to real people. Hamm and Clov, for example, represent opposing psychological tendencies. Thus it would be misleading to think of them as fully developed personalities. And other plays, such as *Death of a Salesman* or *Streetcar Named Desire*, which are admittedly more "realistic" do not embody completely real people. Willy and Blanche, the main characters in each of these plays, do represent complex studies in abnormal psychology, but they are conceived in order to dramatize specific theories about the impact of society upon the individual. Thus they exhibit patterns of behavior which are typical, rather than real.

Although dramatic characters are not real people, they are endowed with human capacities. They talk and act and interact with one another. They experience pleasure and endure pain. They feel, and they act on their feelings. They believe, and they act according to their beliefs. Thus it would be inhuman of us not to respond to their humanity. But we can only respond appropriately if we know what we are responding to. This means that in studying characters we have to consider all the ways in which they are revealed and defined by dialogue and plot.

The most immediate way to understand a character is to examine in detail everything he says. The style and content of his utterances will reveal not only his dominant traits but also the more subtle aspects of his character. As an example of the analysis this requires, reread our discussion of the dialogue between Alceste and Philinte. Another way is to examine what other characters say about him. In *The Misanthrope*, for example, the characters are repeatedly talking about one another—to their faces and behind their backs. Alceste, of course, is the principal topic of conversation, and such characters as Philinte and Éliante provide valuable insights into his behavior. The things a character does will reveal as much about him as what he says and what others say about him. In examining the actions of a character, pay careful attention to context, for characters are likely to behave differently in different situations. The problem in these cases is to determine whether the character has actually changed or not. Consider, for example, the behavior of Oedipus and Hamm. Do they actually change during the course of the play, or is it the case instead that we know them more fully at the end of the play than we did at the beginning. Another important means of understanding a character is to compare and contrast him with other characters in the same play. In order to highlight these relationships, dramatists often take special pains in the construction and arrangement of dramatic units. Thus in the opening unit of *The Misanthrope*, we come to know Alceste not only by what he says and does, but also by contrasting his behavior with that of Philinte. The next dramatic unit shows us Alceste and Oronte, forcing us to make another set of comparisons and contrasts. How do these affect our initial impressions of Alceste and Philinte? In much the same way, Shakespeare invites us to compare and contrast the various lovers and love stories in *A Midsummer-Night's Dream*. To see how this is done, reread our analysis of the first act.

Character analysis of this kind can be a source of pleasure and understanding in its own right. But ultimately it should lead us more deeply into the play as a whole, rather than being an end in itself. Thus when we analyze characters, we should always keep in mind the contexts and modes of drama that shape their being. In this way we will be able to appreciate the dramatic imitation of a world created by the wedding of literary and representational art.